SESAME STREET

WELCOME TO AFGHANISTAN WITH SESAME STREET

CHRISTY PETERSON

Lerner Publications ◆ Minneapolis

In this series, *Sesame Street* characters help readers learn about other countries' people, cultures, landscapes, and more. These books connect friends around the world while giving readers new tools to become smarter, kinder friends. Pack your bags and take a fun-filled look at your world with your funny, furry friends from *Sesame Street*.

—Sincerely, the Editors at Sesame Street

TABLE OF CONTENTS

Welcome to Afghanistan! 4

Where in the World Is Afghanistan? 6

Afghanistan Fast Facts. 21
Glossary 22
Learn More. 23
Index 24

WELCOME TO AFGHANISTAN!

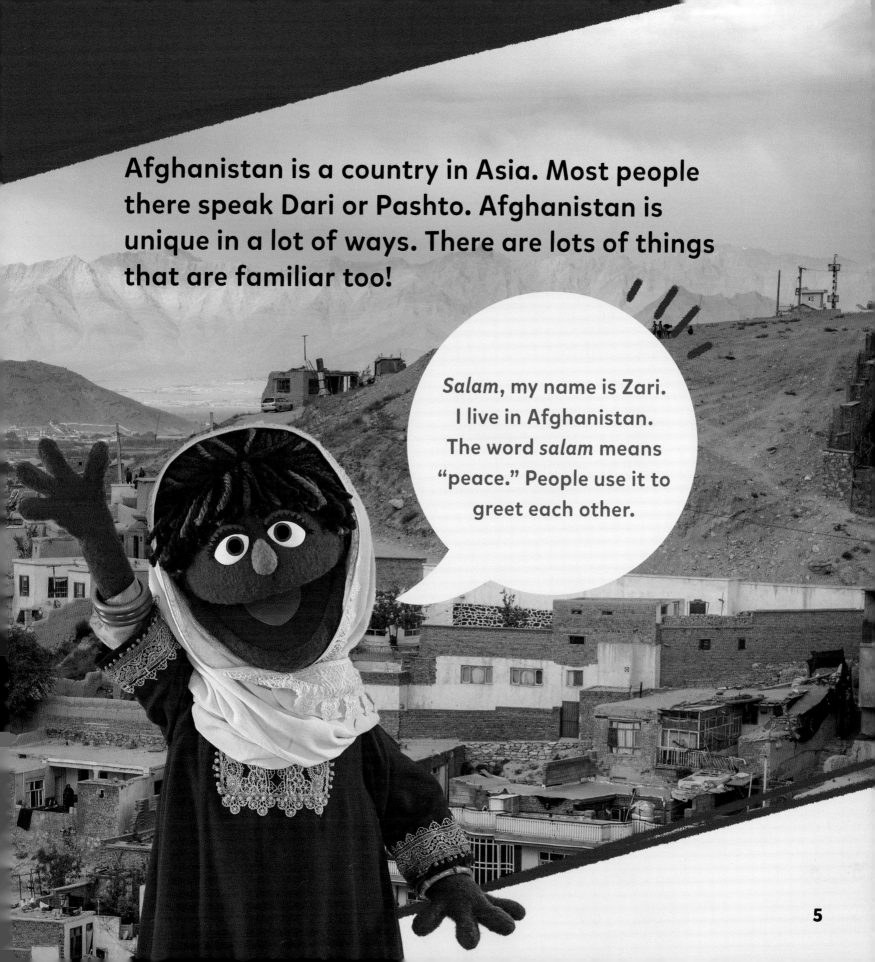

Afghanistan is a country in Asia. Most people there speak Dari or Pashto. Afghanistan is unique in a lot of ways. There are lots of things that are familiar too!

Salam, my name is Zari. I live in Afghanistan. The word *salam* means "peace." People use it to greet each other.

WHERE IN THE WORLD IS AFGHANISTAN?

NORTH AMERICA

ATLANTIC OCEAN

PACIFIC OCEAN

SOUTH AMERICA

UZBEKISTAN

TAJIKISTAN

TURKMENISTAN

Kabul
★

AFGHANISTAN

N

Miles
0   500   1000   1500

0   1000   2000
Kilometers

IRAN

PAKISTAN

Afghanistan and Surrounding Area

ARCTIC OCEAN

ASIA

EUROPE

Afghanistan

AFRICA

PACIFIC OCEAN

INDIAN OCEAN

AUSTRALIA

SOUTHERN OCEAN

The weather in Afghanistan is usually dry. There are flat plains and huge mountains. Band-e Amir National Park has six beautiful blue lakes.

Most people live in villages. They shop at small stores and outdoor markets. You can buy beautiful rugs or tasty food.

Ramadan is an important time for Muslims. Practicing kindness is a tradition during Ramadan. People donate to charities and give food to those in need.

Children often walk to school with their friends. They start the school day by reading poems in front of their class.

Visiting with family and friends is important in Afghanistan. They have tea and snacks together.

Families share food from a large bowl. They enjoy meat, rice, veggies, dumplings, and a flatbread called naan.

My family likes to eat together too.

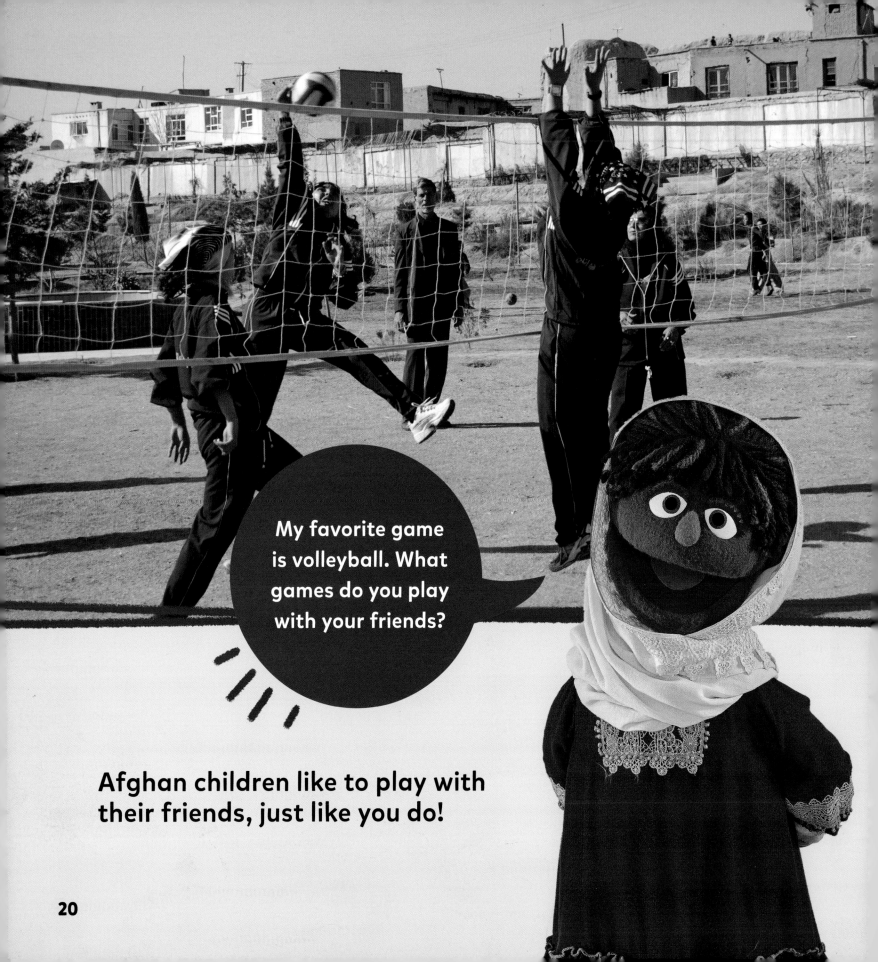

My favorite game is volleyball. What games do you play with your friends?

Afghan children like to play with their friends, just like you do!

20

Flag of Afghanistan

AFGHANISTAN FAST FACTS

Continent: Asia

Capital city: Kabul

Population: 32.9 million

Languages: Dari and Pashto

GLOSSARY

bolani: a flatbread that is filled with foods such as potatoes, leeks, and more

donate: to give money or goods to support a cause

flatbread: bread that is baked in thin, flat shapes instead of loaves

plain: a large area of flat grassland

village: a community that is usually smaller than a town

LEARN MORE

Birdoff, Ariel Factor. *Afghanistan*. New York: Bearport, 2020.

Murray, Julie. *Afghanistan*. Minneapolis: Big Buddy Books, 2016.

Schur, Maxine Rose. *Brave with Beauty: A Story of Afghanistan*. Clifton Park, New York: Yali, 2019.

INDEX

mountains, 8

naan, 18

pomegranates, 9

Ramadan, 12–13

volleyball, 20

Photo Acknowledgments

Additional image credits: mbrand85/Shutterstock.com, pp. 4-5; Laura Westlund/Independent Picture Service, pp. 6-7, 21; Sgt. Ken Scar/US Army/Wikimedia Commons, p. 8; Kakoli Dey/Shutterstock.com, p. 9; Marion Kaplan/Alamy Stock Photo, p. 10; Wasim Abbas 02/Shutterstock.com, p. 11; Feroze Edassery/Shutterstock.com, pp. 12, 17; Reuters/Alamy Stock Photo, pp. 13, 14; Morsalfa/Shutterstock.com, p. 16; Rahmat Gul/AP/Shutterstock.com, p. 18; Lizette Potgieter/Shutterstock.com, p. 20.

Cover: Jono Photography/Shutterstock.com (top), Mushtaq B/Shutterstock.com (bottom).

Lerner Publications Company
An imprint of Lerner Publishing Group, Inc.
241 First Avenue North
Minneapolis, MN 55401 USA

For reading levels and more information, look up this title at www.lernerbooks.com.

Main body text set in Mikido a.
Typeface provided by HVD Fonts.

Editor: Andrea Nelson **Photo Editor:** Brianna Kaiser
Lerner team: Martha Kranes

Library of Congress Cataloging-in-Publication Data

Names: Peterson, Christy, author.
Title: Welcome to Afghanistan with Sesame Street / Christy Peterson.
Description: Minneapolis : Lerner Publications, [2022] | Series: Sesame Street friends around the world | Includes bibliographical references and index. | Audience: Ages 4–8 | Audience: Grades K–1 | Summary: "Afghanistan is a country in South Asia known for its beautiful landscape. Friends from Sesame Street introduce readers to the country, from its tall mountains to its plentiful food markets"– Provided by publisher.
Identifiers: LCCN 2020046115 (print) | LCCN 2020046116 (ebook) | ISBN 9781728424392 (library binding) | ISBN 9781728431505 (paperback) | ISBN 9781728430492 (ebook)
Subjects: LCSH: Afghanistan—Juvenile literature. | Afghanistan—Social life and customs—Juvenile literature. | Sesame Street (Television program)—Juvenile literature.
Classification: LCC DS351.5 .P48 2022 (print) | LCC DS351.5 (ebook) | DDC 958.1—dc23

LC record available at https://lccn.loc.gov/2020046115
LC ebook record available at https://lccn.loc.gov/2020046116

Manufactured in the United States of America
1-49309-49425-4/6/2021